Ten percent of the proceeds from Let's Meet Chicago will go to the following local charities or local chapters of national charities. Each nonprofit was chosen by the family or child who is profiled in the following pages.

- NAMI Chicago (namichicago.org)
- Urban Prep Academies (urbanprep.org)
- Open Books (open-books.org)
- Planned Parenthood of Illinois (plannedparenthood.org)
- Autism Speaks Chicago & Wisconsin (autismspeaks.org)
- I Grow Chicago (igrowchicago.org)
- Enlace Chicago (enlacechicago.org)
- Lurie Children's Hospital of Chicago (luriechildrens.org)
- Cradles to Crayons Chicago (cradlestocrayons.org)
- Coming Up Rosies (cominguprosies.com)
- Gilda's Club Chicago (gildasclubchicago.org)
- National Alumnae Association of Spelman College – Chicago Chapter (naasc-chicago.org)
- HIAS Chicago (hiaschicago.org)
- Saint Henry Catholic Church (sainthenrychicago.org)

# Let's Meet...and EXPLORE!

My name is Alina, but on the following pages you'll meet: Sophia, Rosie, Caleb, Penny, Dillon, Adam, Micah, Cruz, Finn, Ava, Pareezeh, Nicole, Vikram and Nyla.

(Don't worry -- you won't need to remember all of our names.)

Flip the page (no not now — after you read this note) for a peek into Chicago neighborhoods and the kids who live there.

Every kid in this city makes Chicago special -- and we all share a for this place we call home.

So don't let me keep you. Read on and get to know the lives of some Chi-town kids — one may even be your neighbor.

Then, put down the book and explore some of their neighborhoods. (On every page you'll find suggestions on what to do without spending a dime.)

Love from the Windy City,
Alina

P.S. - You can email the children in this book at letsmeetbooks@gmail.com and I'll forward them your message.

# Sophia

Let's meet Sophia.
She's 6-years-old and lives in Little Village.

**At home:** I watch TV with my little brother Dieguito. But sometimes, he's more interested in playing with blocks.

**For dinner, I eat:** Tamales — they are made from corn and the stuff inside is so good.

**The animal I'd want to be is:** A bat. I like being awake in the dark. I don't like going to sleep. And I'd like to fly sometimes.

**If I could go anywhere, I'd go to:** New York. They have an M&Ms store.

**In my dreams:** I do karate.

**I'm special because:** I know three languages. I learn Mandarin at school and my grandma speaks to me in Spanish.

Tip:
Wander 26TH Street and save room for some tasty paletas.

# Cruz

Let's meet Cruz.
He is 7-years-old and lives in Lincoln Square.

**In my house:** I like my grandma's room. It's empty, but sometimes she comes to visit from Costa Rica.

**On Sundays:** I play flag football. Last year, we were the Packers, now our team is the Bears. I still have both jerseys.

**I like:** To do equations. Math is my favorite.

**In the city:** I go to the Shedd Aquarium. I love the show where you get to see the dolphins and whales. I like to sit and watch it from up high.

**At restaurants I eat:** Sushi. I get the Dragon roll because it has eel and I like to put salt on the edamame. At other restaurants, my favorite is squid and octopus.

**My friends ask me to:** Tie shoes. I was the first one to learn how to do it and usually have to tie everybody's shoes in school. Sometimes I do double knots.

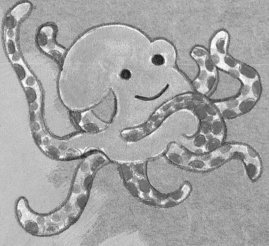

Tip:
Belt out some tunes
during a concert
at the Welles Park
gazebo.

# Penny

**Let's meet Penny.**
**She is 11-years-old and lives in Woodlawn**

**At school:** I'm in theater. We're doing Aladdin and I'm singing as part of Prince Ali's entourage. My school is Chinatown, which means that on Chinese New Year we always have a big assembly.

**On the weekends:** I like going to the farmer's market near our house. I always get Asian pears when they are there because they are crunchier than regular ones.

**My friends:** Have about 8 siblings or more. I'm glad to only have one sister, Carly, even though she feels like 10 sisters.

**People don't know this, but:** I'm not much of a hugger -- I just don't like hugs that much.

**I love:** Dictionaries. I always read them and look for new words. Right now, it's the word 'forethought' which means to think about the future.

hippopotamus

Tip:
Pack the binoculars
and go bird watching
in Jackson Park.

# Adam

Let's meet Adam.
He is 10-years-old and lives in Norwood Park.

**In my house:** I share a room with my brothers, Amir and Rayyan. We make forts on my bed -- we use three covers and six pillows.

**For lunch, I bring:** zeit ou za'atar on bread. When you put olive oil on za'atar spice blend, it turns green. My classmates like to see it.

**I wish:** I could go on an airplane. I always see planes in the air and wonder if they are looking down at us.

**I admire:** My dad. He works hard to pay for our house and I don't see him at home a lot.

**My favorite holiday is:** Eid. We fast for a whole month and come together as a family — even my cousins.

**I'm special because:** I actually like doing homework. It helps me get more knowledge.

**Tip:**
Tour the Noble-Seymour-Crippen House, rumored to be the oldest in the city.

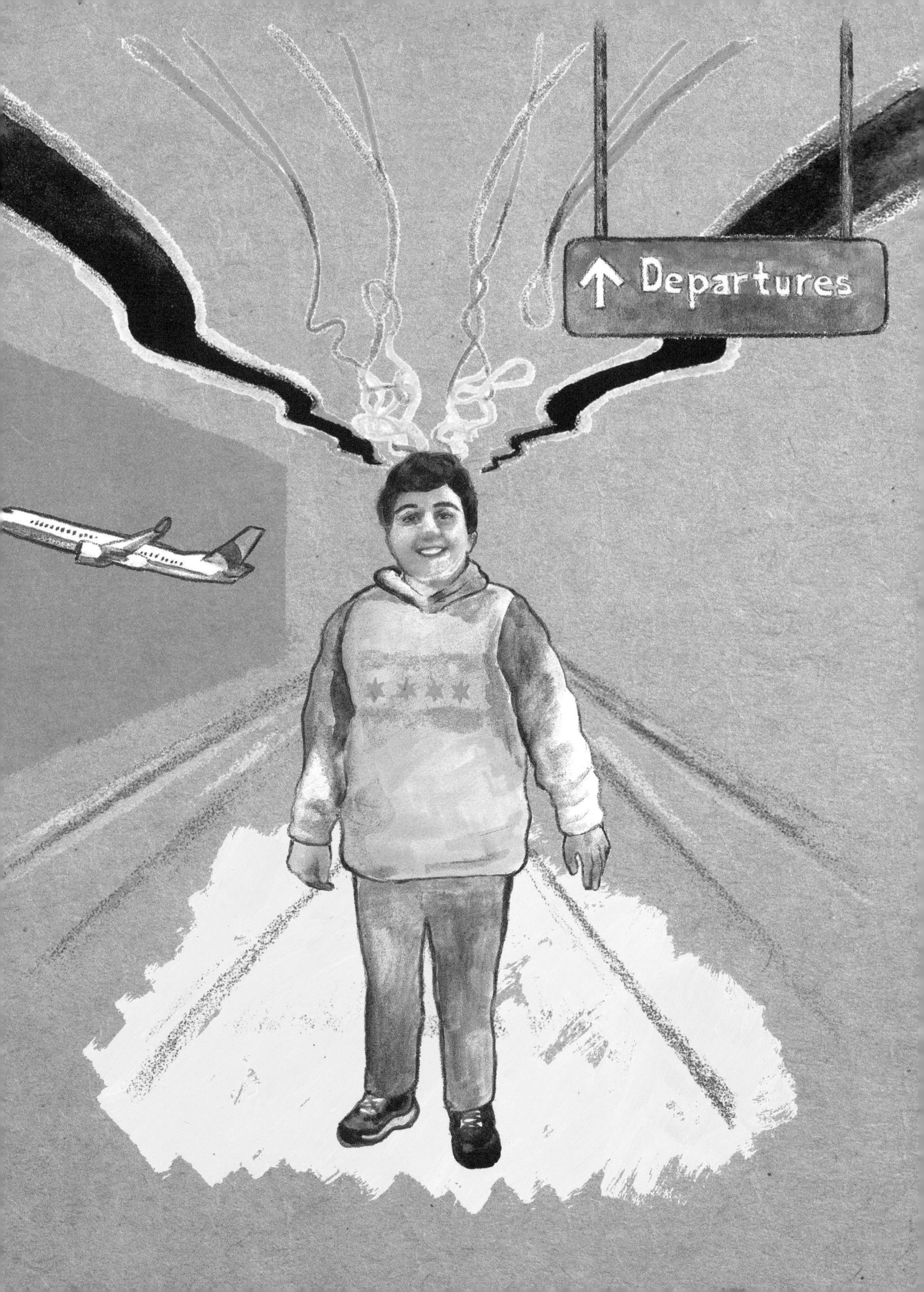
↑ Departures

# Finn

Let's meet Finn.
He is 10-years-old and lives in Wicker Park.

**Our dog's name is:** Gatsby. I like petting him whenever I'm freaking out. It basically relieves stress, and he's soft, so why not? At first, my sister Skye and I wanted to name him Chicken.

**For dinner:** I like my mom's tacos and my other mom's Romanian soup -- it's a bitter version of chicken noodle soup.

**At school:** I'm always racing with my friends and I've been playing kickball. I like competitive things.

**I admire:** My parents. I call them mommy and mama. I wouldn't even be alive if it wasn't for them. It's like I won the lottery.

**I'm special because:** I won the spelling bee last year. In the end, I got a fairly easy word — S-N-O-B-B-E-R-Y. We have it on camera.

**Tip:**
Step inside the Flatiron Arts Building to get your creative juices flowing.

# Dillon

Let's meet Dillon.
She is 7-years-old and lives in Lakeshore East.

**When I'm excited:** I do my happy dance. I look like a chicken jumping and my hands are flapping by my sides. It takes a lot of my energy out. Sometimes I do it when I get wiggle breaks during a long test at school.

**In the park:** I always go on the swings. At first I wasn't able to swing and I needed someone to push me. Now, I start from low to high, and sometimes I'm half way up in the air.

**For fun:** I like singing, ballet and Taekwondo. I also go sailing on Lake Michigan. But when it's cold on the water, I want to go back inside in like five minutes.

**At home:** I could see the John Hancock building and I like seeing all the little people that look like ants running. Whenever I'm sad, I go to my room -- so I'm not always out in public.

**Tip:**
Explore all the action on the banks of the Chicago River.

# Nicole

**Let's meet Nicole.**
She is 11-years-old and lives in Lincoln Park.

**On the weekends:** I really like walking around the city. With my mom's camera I take pictures of the Lincoln Park Zoo and around the Nature Museum.

**I'd want to tell others that:** I'm so lucky to have so many things, but if you don't do anything to help others it doesn't mean anything.

**On weekends:** I've been having sleepovers since I was little. My parents are not overprotective at all.

**At my school:** There are leadership opportunities. I was in Student Council this year. Next year I may run for Secretary.

**My favorite holiday is:** Hanukkah. We light the candles and we also get lots of presents. The presents are nice, but that's not the meaning of the holiday.

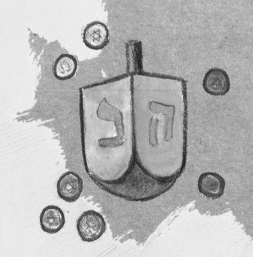

Tip:
Find a green retreat from the city at the Lincoln Park Conservatory.

# Micah

Let's meet Micah.
He is six-years-old and lives in Washington Heights.

**At home:** There are a lot of hiding spots. I have a secret hiding spot in the kitchen cabinets — I can squeeze in there. Other times, I hide in my daddy's closet behind his ties.

**It's annoying:** When my sister Tesah drools on me.

**On Halloween:** I was a wizard. Next year, I want to be very scary and look like I have an eyeball poked out.

**Outside:** I like to make a snowman. First I just make a mountain, then the body, and then I put rocks and sticks to make the face. No carrot -- I only use stuff that you can find outside.

**I speak:** A little bit of Czech, English and French, but I want to know Spanish like my cousin.

**I'm special because:** I have a strawberry birthmark. It looks like a strawberry and I think it's what makes me super fast. I also like to eat strawberries a lot.

**Tip:**
Bike or skate along the tree-lined Major Taylor Trail.

# Ava

Let's meet Ava.

She is eight-years-old and lives in Logan Square.

**On weekends:** I like going to climb in Maggie Daley [Park]. It looks like a castle. Last time, we played on the slides. The tall slides are taller than our house.

**At school:** I like playing basketball. Soon, I'll be on the basketball team, but I need to practice.

**In science class:** We made oobleck. It's liquid but when you punch it, it turns solid.

**I want to learn about:** The narwhal. I've only seen them in pictures. It's a whale and they have a long horn that looks like a unicorn.

**As the oldest:** I have a lot of responsibilities. I help my brother Peter with homework and my other brother Paul to put on Barbie clothes. Paul is a big fan of Barbie.

**I'm special because:** My entire family thinks I'm a really good writer. They also like how I smile a lot.

Tip:
Stroll the elevated 606 trail and get a glimpse of the city from up high.

# Rosie

Let's meet Rosie.
She is six-years-old and lives in Lakeview.

**In my room:** I have an owl. It's a toy my younger sister Caroline got when she was little. Now she wants it back. But I'm like 'Look, I get to keep it, it's mine.'

**I'm learning:** Piano. Playing piano helps you with math -- it's a really cool fact.

**I like to play:** Softball. During the season we play at Oz Park. We wear visors, but why don't we have baseball hats? My head can get sunburned.

**I get cranky when:** I have to wait in lines. There was a two-hour line to see Santa. It made me mad out of my pants.

**In the winter:** I like to go ice-skating at Wrigley Field. In the summertime, we play outside Wrigley in the fountains.

**I'm special because:** When I first didn't have something to protect my head, because my hair doesn't grow, I wasn't that confident. But then I learned how to be confident and now I have a charity that helps me and other kids.

Tip:
Visit Gallagher Way,
a plaza overlooking
Wrigley Field -- no
ticket required.

# Caleb

**Let's meet Caleb.**
**He is 10-years-old and lives in Hyde Park.**

**At home:** My dad fixes things like lights and electronics and like pipes or something. He's also a surgeon. But I don't want to be a doctor like him, because there's too much blood.

**In fourth grade:** We had to identify rocks in science class, but everybody hated it. Then we had a play about the Civil Rights Movement, but some of the fifth and sixth graders messed up.

**In the afternoons:** I go to my grandma's house. Her house is kind of small and it's also really hot there. Being with her is fun and she does a lot of funny things.

**I play:** Soccer. It's a way to meet new people and show your skills. I want to go see the Chicago Fire play.

**I'm different because:** I'm the shortest kid in my class. I get made fun of a lot, but I don't really care because I can do things other people can't, like fit through things. It's not that bad being short.

**My best friend's name is:** Ale. He's really nice and he's really good at soccer and he's got my back if somebody is picking on me.

Tip:
Get your history
fix at the DuSable
Museum — it's free on
Tuesdays.

# Pareezeh

Let's meet Pareezeh.
She is 9-years-old and lives in Albany Park.

**At home:** I help my mom clean the dishes and the house. I remind my parents about something if they forget. Sometimes my mom forgets about laundry.

**When I wake up:** I look out the window. The people walking below show me how I should be dressed and if it's cold or warm. The tree tells me how windy it is. In my country it was always warm.

**Near our house:** There's a river where you can see ducks and some boats. My brother and I like to ride our bikes downhill.

**To eat:** I like chicken wings. And some good sandwiches with peanut butter and jelly or strawberry jam. And macaroni without cheese.

**For fun:** I like to make my own books. Sometimes, I write horror stories about knocks on the door.

**I moved here:** from Pakistan. I had lots of friends over there. Here, I only have two friends so far and I have not had that many play dates. There I had the biggest funnest birthday and over here it was small -- but it was kind of nice.

Tip:
Spot the wildlife as you follow the river through Ronan Park.

# Vikram

Let's meet Vikram.
He is six-years-old and lives in the Loop.

**At home:** I have an office — it's diagonal to my daddy's office. I usually play or write in my diary. I don't allow anyone in there besides my mom.

**For breakfast:** I eat homemade scrambled eggs and toast with butter that daddy makes. He is the world's best butter spreader on toast.

**In class:** we started using real money. I'm the best at money. We played a game with it and everyone said, "You're the best!"

**At Navy Pier:** I love to ride on the Ferris wheel. It spins around and you can see the whole Chicago. I always take a selfie with my mom's phone. It's fun, but when it goes fast, it's a little worrying.

**I love:** Speed stacking. It's where you have to stack cups super fast and the most hardest thing is to balance them. I'm the state champion. I can run really fast too.

**I learned that:** if you're nice to people, they will respect you. Then you will respect yourself when you grow up.

Tip:
Splash in the
Crown Fountain in
Millenium Park --
shoes optional.

# Nyla

**Let's meet Nyla.**
**She is seven-years-old and lives in Rogers Park.**

**When I was little:** I spoke Vietnamese and I didn't know English. I learned English from my neighbor. At home I still speak Vietnamese with my ba ngoai and ong ngoai because my grandma and grandpa don't speak English.

**Saturdays:** We go to church with my family. Sometimes I like it. This summer, there was a festival with cotton candy.

**Afterward:** I go to Argyle [Street]. I get the colorful bubble tea and the stretchy rolls called banh cuon.

**At school:** We had slime class. We made all kinds of slime, even fluffy slime. But when I played with it at home, my little brother was scared of it and ran away.

**I run around at:** Indian Boundary Park. The monkey bars are close together, so I can skip one or two when I go across. On the slides it's boring, because you just sit; on the monkey bars you get to swing.

**I have:** My own YouTube channel. It's where I read books that my teacher assigns. At the end of the videos, I didn't know what to say, so my dad had to write it on paper. Now I say: "Thank you for watching, make sure you like and subscribe."

Tip:
Explore Loyola University's lakefront campus with a picnic in hand.

# Now it's *your* turn!

Try it out: Find a Chicagoan who is exactly your age, but make sure the person lives in a neighborhood that's different from the one you live in. Ask the person the questions below and fill-in the blanks.

My name is _____ and I'm ___-years-old.

I live in _____.

At home, my favorite place to hang out is:

During school, I always:

My friends would describe me as:

If I could do anything, I would:

My magic powers are:

I'm never happy when:

I'm always talking about:

I'm special because:

Draw the person who answered the questions with some of the things mentioned in the answers above on the opposite page.

A (personal) note from the author:

I grew up in Chicago, but emigrated from Kharkov (in what's now Ukraine) as a second grader. Feeling accepted by my elementary classmates was difficult. There were tears. And I often felt isolated from the rest of the city.

Fast forward a few decades and I'm now raising my children in Chicago. (Hi Anais and Theo!) My goal is for beginning readers to understand how to celebrate the diversity of this city without shying away from challenging topics.

With that in mind, I traversed the city by train, car and bus to meet the kids of Chicago. I was welcomed into so many homes by enthusiastic families and feel fortunate to have met amazing children.

This book is a way to begin the dialogue about diversity and inclusion through the eyes of young people as they introduce themselves and their neighborhoods. It's a springboard for conversation -- a way to discuss what it means to look, feel, act or believe differently from the people around us. It's a tiny step forward to celebrating our differences.

A bit about my process: As a professional journalist, I approached writing this book as I did an article. I met with all of the children illustrated on these pages for formal face-to-face interviews inside their homes. Their answers are only edited for clarity and reflect the diversity that gives Chicago its power. I worked with the talented illustrator Sonja Oldenburg whose art made the pages come to life.

The result is an accessible way to applaud diversity for some of our youngest readers and to encourage them to go out and explore.

Thanks for joining me on this journey!
Alina